Unique

Contents

A Letter from Alison Allen-Gray	3
A Day in the Life of…	4–5
Back to the Future 	6
Run to the Hills	7
Boy Wonder!	8–9
Happy Birthday Two Ewe!	10–13
Hackmail!	14–15
Pathways… to Another Good Read	16

Great Clarendon Street, Oxford OX2 6DP

Oxford University Press is a department of the University of Oxford.
It furthers the University's objective of excellence in research, scholarship,
and education by publishing worldwide in

Oxford   New York

Auckland   Cape Town   Dar es Salaam   Hong Kong   Karachi
Kuala Lumpur   Madrid   Melbourne   Mexico City   Nairobi
New Delhi   Shanghai   Taipei   Toronto

With offices in

Argentina   Austria   Brazil   Chile   Czech Republic   France   Greece
Guatemala   Hungary   Italy   Japan   South Korea   Poland   Portugal
Singapore   Switzerland   Thailand   Turkey   Ukraine   Vietnam

Oxford is a registered trade mark of Oxford University Press
in the UK and in certain other countries

© Helen Field-Mears 2006

The moral rights of the author have been asserted

Database right Oxford University Press (maker)

First published 2006

All rights reserved. No part of this publication may be reproduced,
stored in a retrieval system, or transmitted, in any form or by any means,
without the prior permission in writing of Oxford University Press,
or as expressly permitted by law, or under terms agreed with the appropriate
reprographics rights organization. Enquiries concerning reproduction
outside the scope of the above should be sent to the Rights Department,
Oxford University Press, at the address above

You must not circulate this book in any other binding or cover
and you must impose this same condition on any acquirer

British Library Cataloguing in Publication Data

Data available

ISBN-13: 978-019-832651-9

ISBN-10: 0-19-832651-3

10 9 8 7 6 5 4 3 2

Printed in Malaysia by Imago.

Acknowledgements

P5t Bob Krist/Corbis; **p5b** Digital Vision/OUP; **p6** Ace Stock Limited/Alamy; **p7** Fine Art Photographic Library/Corbis; **p11t**; Corbis RF; **p11b** Reuters/Corbis; **p12l** Rick Friedman/Corbis; **p12r** Reuters/Corbis; **p13** Kim Kulish/Corbis; **p14** Photodisc/OUP.

Illustrations are by John Hallett **pp 6, 8m, 10, 11, 13, 14** and Chris King **pp 4, 8t&b. 9**.

We are grateful for permission to reprint the following copyright material in this guide:

Alison Allen-Gray: letter used by permission of the author.

CNN: extracts from news reports dated 12.2.04 and 27.12.04 from www.cnn.com, reprinted by permission of CNN.

Robin McKie: 'Dolly the Sheep creator turns to humans', *The Observer*, 13.10.02, copyright © Guardian Newspapers Ltd 2002, reprinted by permission of GNL.

We have tried to trace and contact all copyright holders before publication. If notified, the publisher will be pleased to rectify any errors or omissions at the earliest opportunity.

Key to icons:

 Pair or group activity

 A resources sheet from the Teacher's Pack supports this activity.

A Letter from Alison Allen-Gray

Dear Readers,

Back in 1997, I was at a party held by our writers' group, Islington Writers for Children, when someone mentioned a news story about Dolly the sheep. It was this that provided the spark that led to *Unique*.

All that existed of *Unique* at that time was a pile of dry sticks – ideas, sketchy scenes and story plans about a lonely, damaged boy struggling to find his own identity. I was also interested in ideas about control and manipulation. But these aren't exactly original themes, and what I needed was a way of exploring them that nobody had hit upon before – a way to set my pile of sticks roaring into flame.

Once I began to think about what this news story meant, I realized it was the spark I needed. I'd found the new 'twist' to the telling of a tale about identity and control. From that moment on, my central character, Dominic, lived and grew.

My new idea took me into a subject that I knew very little about, so I began some research. For weeks, I delved into piles of books about science and the ethics of science, searching for things I could use. I found loads of facts and opinions and wove many of them into the fabric of the story.

But at the end of the day, a book only works if readers feel close to the characters and *their* personal journeys. Much of a writer's work is structuring a story in a way that is satisfying for the reader. For me, that structure often comes through character. Our actions and reactions reveal who we are. What would *you* do if you made the terrifying discovery that Dominic makes?

Enough said. I hope that you enjoy reading *Unique*, because that, above anything else, is what books are for.

Alison Allen-Gray

A Day in the Life of...Dominic Gordon

One reader's view of Unique

Discuss this short review. It captures one reader's reactions to the storyline and to Dominic, the central character.

> This is a very fast moving and pacy story, told with an exciting and fresh voice.
> It starts really well, with the reader immediately drawn into the mystery of who Dominic really is – by page 13, the reader's hooked.
> Dominic is a likeable character and the reader feels a great deal of sympathy for him and the revelations that he has to try to come to terms with. You admire his strength and determination, and empathize with the wealth of emotions that he feels. You care what happens to him and hope that it will work out for him in the end.

I pulled out the little red book with its gilded school crest and flicked through with trembling fingers to look at the grades.

I was staring at the face of a young man... It was my face looking at me. A few years older, but my face. But it couldn't be!

This wasn't the answer I'd wanted... Something in her eyes – the terror, pain, whatever it was, gave me a clue.

It's all about you!

What a day! Dominic's dad is bitterly disappointed, his granddad holds a secret, his mother is terrified and it's all about him. But Allen-Gray thinks it's all about you, too! Swap stories with your partner about your feelings when you:

- were disappointed or disappointed someone else
- had to keep a secret
- realized your parents have feelings too.

of...Dominic Gordon

Dominic's family tree

Pops (Mr Richardson) m. Gran
|
(daughter) Carla Richardson m. Michael Gordon
|
(1st son) – Dominic Michael Gordon —— (2nd son) – Dominic Michael Gordon
(died Feb. 2001)   (born 1st Jan. 2002)

Intriguing documents

In Cambridge, Dominic finds two old postcards written to Giles – one from his mum and one from Nick. Much later in the story, he witnesses numerous confidential files being burned by Professor Holt...

CONFIDENTIAL

Property of Professor Imogen Holt

Dearest Giles,
I have never written to thank you for your kindness when Nick died. Please forgive me, but things have been terrible these last few weeks. As you can see, we are now in the Cayman Islands at the generous invitation of Professor Holt, who is here doing some research and kindly thought that the break might do us good...
All my love, Carla

POST CARD — CAYMAN ISLANDS MAR 2001

Giles Nickalls,
Greneville Hall
Cambridge University

Giles, you old gibbon,
Hurry up and pass those re-sits and get yourself down here. Pops has been taking us flying and it's FANTASTIC! It turns out that Becky has a talent for it (flying I mean!) and Pops has let her take the controls already... Please don't think you'll be a gooseberry, because you won't be – we all want you here, so GET ON WITH IT!
Nick

POST CARD — HARTFORD JULY 2001

Giles Nickalls,
Greneville Hall
Cambridge University

unique

Back to the Future

Good to be Back

Cambridge University is one of the oldest in the world, celebrating its 800th anniversary in 2009. Earliest records show that, in 1209, scholars met together and began teaching and learning until small colleges formed. (Eventually, doctors grouped themselves into 'faculties' of different subjects — such as Philosophy, Medicine, Literature and Mathematics to name but a few.)

So the University is made up of over thirty different colleges, each with their own grounds and buildings each including chapels, libraries and museums. One even has its own cathedral! Students live in the ancient colleges, have their own room to sleep and study in and eat together in the great hall. Anyone can apply to go to Cambridge University, but you have to be clever to be offered a place. And, if you study at Cambridge, you often have a lesson with your teacher on your own! How scary is that? Also, there are many traditions from the past still held today, for example, some colleges do not admit women students!

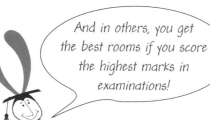

And in others, you get the best rooms if you score the highest marks in examinations!

Web Cam

The city of Cambridge is very picturesque, lying on the River Cam, where many people walk, picnic or even take a punt down stream – not as easy as it looks! It's not a bit like the famous annual Oxford-Cambridge boat race.

10 Ways to Find More Time!

- What evidence can you find of old Cambridge in the novel? Find four or five references which Allen-Gray makes to the Cambridge of **the past**.
- How does she suggest that the novel is set in **the future**? Are there inventions, services or products which Dominic uses which we don't have yet?

Fill-in your ideas on a Time Train line like the one below.

Run to the Hills!
...Run for Your Life!

Get Away from it All
Need to get away from it all? Go where no one knows you? Where no one can find you? There are plenty of places to hide...

Give us the Goss!
Imagine you need to escape – and soon, yesterday, if possible!
- Where would you run?
- How would you get there?
- Would you tell anyone where you were going?
- What would you take with you?

Scotland – the Tops
You wouldn't be the first if you chose Scotland for your hiding place. Scotland tops Britain with two thirds of its land being mountains – composed of the Highlands, the Central Lowlands and the Southern Uplands. Of course, there are also the magnificent lochs and fabulously empty, white-sand beaches. This Celtic land has been a haven for those who want to find an escape from the world throughout time. From Bonny Prince Charlie to eloping couples, people have run to find sanctuary in this magical and awesome landscape. So what are you waiting for? Go pack your bags!

Pretty as a Picture!
One way to do justice to Scotland's landscape is to recreate it in a work of art. And that is just what so many artists and writers have done – in painting or through poetry.

> The heath waves wild upon her hills,
> Her foaming frae the fells,
> Her fountains sing o' freedom still,
> As they dance down the dells.
> And weel I loe the land, my lads,
> That's girded by the sea.
> Then Scotland's vales, and Scotland's dales,
> And Scotland's hills for me;
> I'll drink a cup to Scotland yet,
> Wi a' the honours three!
>
> Henry Scott Riddell

Quick Quiz
Re-read the paragraph on page 202 of *Unique*, beginning 'I was climbing now...'
1. What verbs suggest that it is difficult to climb the mountain?
2. What adjectives give a sense of danger to the cliff and the lake?

Unique

Boy Wonder!

One in a billion

Boy-bands, teenage heroes, eye-candy for the girls: they're all special, but are they as unique as we think? May be not! But here's one who's truly one in a billion – our very own wonder-boy in every sense!

Fact file

Name	Dominic Gordon
Age	Fifteen
D.o.B	01/01/2002
Star sign	Capricorn
Best subject	Art
Worst subjects	Chemistry and Physics
Family	Dad (Michael Gordon) – Owner/Director of Gordon's Pharmaceuticals
	Mother (Carla Gordon) – Once a famous opera singer
	Brother (Dominic Michael Gordon a.k.a. Nick) – Cambridge star Graduate
Hobbies	Painting, personal mysteries, buying chocolate doughnuts
Favourite people	Pops, Giles and Becky
Favourite animal	Caliban (pet cat)
Best thing that ever happened	Discovering he had a brother
Worst thing that ever happened	Discovering he had a brother
Ambition	Painting landscapes and animals in Australia
Celeb status	Human clone

I wonder, I wa, wa, wa, wa, wonder

By Chapter 18, Dominic is beginning to wonder who he really is. Everyone else seems to have an opinion on the subject, as you can see in the talking heads below!

- Discuss the feelings each character has about Dominic.
- What do these feelings tell you about each of their relationships with Dominic?

[Michael Gordon:] I do not want the embarrassment of a son for whom I have to apologize the whole time!

[Carla Gordon:] He's MY CHILD! We've hurt him!

8

Wonder!

Clone alone – exclusive interview!

Well… of a sort! We put to Dominic the questions you're all dying to ask – but what did he say? Choose the answers he gave by finding quotations to prove how well you know him.

Part One (Chapters 1–22)

1. How did you feel when you first found out about Nick? (Chapter 2)
   a Excited
   b Disbelieving
   c Angry

2. Did you feel the same person when you discovered you had a brother? (Chapter 3)
   a Completely different!
   b I didn't know who I really was.
   c It didn't make any difference!

3. Would you swap your parents if you could? (Chapters 1 and 7)
   a Neither of them
   b My mum
   c My dad
   d Both

4. What did you feel when you first realized you were cloned? (Chapters 21 and 22)
   a Shocked
   b Angry
   c Confused
   d All of the above!

Part Two (Chapters 23–45)

5. Do you think human cloning is a good idea? (Chapter 38)
   a I think it is a very frightening experience.
   b A good idea – everyone can live forever.
   c A bad idea – it's not natural.

6. Why did your dad have Nick cloned? (Chapters 27 and 30)
   a He was so upset at Nick's death.
   b He thinks he can fix any problem.
   c He wanted to make my mother happy.

7. Why did your mum agree to have Nick cloned? (Chapter 27)
   a She wanted her trophy son back.
   b Her grief was too much to bear.
   c She was persuaded by her husband.

8. Would you swap your parents now? (Chapters 27, 39, 40)
   a Neither of them
   b My mum
   c My dad
   d Both

9. Do you feel special? (Chapter 45)
   a Yes
   b No
   c Everyone is unique.

[Giles:] Dominic's father shouldn't compare him with Nick. His father's very wrong to put that sort of pressure on him… I think Nick would be bowled over by the idea of having a brother, if he could know.

[Professor Holt:] Dominic has an exceptional talent! His technical ability alone is extraordinary…

[Becky:] Being around Dominic wrong-foots me sometimes because there are moments when I remember so clearly what it was like to be eighteen and in love.

Unique

Happy Birthday Two Ewe!

Lambing time

In 1996, at the Roslin Institute in Scotland, the first animal was cloned: a sheep. This little lamb, called Dolly, fuelled an already fiery debate about the rights and wrongs of genetic engineering. Of course, the most controversial aspect of such scientific research is animal cloning and at last it had been achieved. Animal cloning is very difficult – in fact, most of the time it fails to work! Plants can be cloned relatively easily.

Did you know that in the early 1900s, a Bartlett Pear was cloned? There was very little public concern!

Some bacteria can be cloned, but a mammal is a greater challenge. Thirteen sheep underwent the same procedure as Dolly's surrogate mother when Dolly was cloned. None of them produced a lamb.

Blinded by science?

Don't be! It may be difficult to put into practice, but the theory is relatively simple. (Perhaps that's why everyone is so concerned about it!) Here's how it happened.

Stage 1
An udder cell (a somatic cell) was taken from Sheep A – the donor sheep – and cultured for several weeks to reach a state of 'arrest' – in other words, it had a rest from doing whatever it is cells do! Then an unfertilized egg was taken from Sheep B.

Stage 2
The DNA from the egg was removed so that it had no genetic code of its own and no nucleus. The somatic cell could then be fused with the egg – with a bit of help from electricity!

Stage 3
The egg then began to divide – forming an embryo. This was implanted into the uterus of Sheep C who gave birth 142 days later.

Dolly was an exact copy of donor Sheep A.

Birthday Two Ewe!

Spot the difference!
What is the biggest difference between the cloning of Dolly and Dominic?

It's all news to me!
The debate about cloning rumbles on. Often, the media focuses on its most sensational aspects. This is fuelled by the increasing possibility that humans will be cloned. So, what do you think?

Look at the newspaper article below and on pages 12–13. Talk about them. Dip into the *Think tank* on page 12 for some key questions you might like to consider..

See the answer at the bottom of the page.

Professor Ian Wilmut, creator of Dolly the Sheep, is planning to clone human embryos, it was revealed yesterday. The biologist disclosed that he was preparing to lodge Britain's first application to carry out highly controversial stem-cell research on humans.

Wilmut, of the Roslin Institute in Edinburgh, said that, if his institute approved the idea, it would then be considered by external regulators.

If given the green light, the professor's research would focus on using the same technique that was used to create Dolly – nuclear transfer – to clone early human embryos. The cells would be genetically identical to cells taken from an adult. More important, these embryonic stem cells would act as parent cells that could develop into any type of tissue.

Quick Quiz
Got the facts straight? Let's check:
1. Which sheep supplied the somatic cell?
2. Where did the egg come from?
3. Why was Dolly a clone of Sheep A?

Answer: The somatic cell was taken from Nick when he was dead and from Sheep A when it was alive!

unique

The leader of a religious sect that claimed to have created the first human clone called the development 'just the first step' toward human immortality...

Claude Vorilhon, 'Rael', claims to be a direct descendant of extraterrestrials who created human life on Earth through genetic engineering. A company founded by his followers announced... that the first human clone has been born – a 7-pound baby girl dubbed 'Eve'.

The announcement was met with scepticism... since other cloned mammals have had serious birth defects or developed health problems. But... Rael dismissed concerns saying, 'What if the child is perfectly healthy and beautiful? I think opponents to cloning are more afraid of that than of the faults.'

Brigitte Boisselier, chief executive officer of the Raelian-founded company, Clonaid, said Eve... is a genetic twin of her mother, a 31-year-old American citizen.

'The best proof that we can have is probably the grandmother, who said she looked just like the mother...'.

The Raelians eventually hope to develop adult clones into which humans could transfer their brains. Rael said, 'Cloning a baby is just the first step... my ultimate goal is to give humanity eternal life through cloning.'

The announcement was followed by criticism from Dr Robert Lanza of Advanced Cell Technologies. He said, 'One has to be very, very skeptical. This is a group that has no scientific track record. They have never published a single scientific paper in this area, they have no research experience in this area. In fact, they have never even cloned a mouse or a rabbit. I have to say that I think this is appalling and scientifically irresponsible... We should not dismiss them outright; we do have the technology at present to clone human embryos and it may be a lot easier than many scientists think.'

Cc the copycat!

An announcement that scientists in Texas have successfully cloned the world's first domestic cat has met with a mixed response. The two-month-old kitten – called Carbon copy, or Cc for short – is healthy and energetic, giving hope to owners who want to recreate a lost pet. However, creating Cc was not a simple exercise – she is the only successful outcome from 87 kitten embryos produced by cloning. And the same team has been trying unsuccessfully for several years to clone a dog.

They were funded by billionaire John Sperling whose dream is to reproduce his much loved border-collie, Missy. Sperling also backs a private company, Texas based Genetic Savings and Clone who already offer a service to wealthy pet owners, freezing DNA from cats and dogs ready for the day when pet cloning is a reality.

Critics, however, are alarmed at the development, believing the cute and loveable Cc brings the public perception of cloning closer to home, and so increases the acceptability of human embryo cloning.

Despite objections from religious groups and doubts about the many abnormalities experienced by cloned animals, Panayiotis Zavos, a US fertility expert has claimed that cloning can help a small percentage of childless couples to have children of their own. He claims that the desire to help infertile couples is his sole motivation to continue with his controversial work.

Think tank!

- Would you consider cloning your pet?
- What might be the benefits of cloning any type of human tissue?
- What beliefs held by the Raelians cast doubt over their claims?
- Why is cloning humans so 'controversial'?
- Is there any proof that 'Eve' exists?

Second thoughts

How does Allen-Gray use science to convince the reader that Dominic is a clone of Nick?
Reading back over Chapters 20–23 may help you to gather evidence.

Unique

Hackmail!

What ever it takes

Journalists are notorious for their willingness to do anything for a good story. Leanne Kelsey is no different – perhaps worse as she has a personal motive driving her on since Nick's death. She writes in a sensational way about the issue of cloning.

Word up!

Have another look at Leanne's over-the-top, colloquial style (page 205) beginning at 'And if Wishart, an obscure doctor…' to '…in our midst'.
- Which words suggest she is exaggerating?
- Which words show that she is biased?
- Where does she try to stir strong emotions in the reader?

Hacking it

Journalists who write just for the money are called 'hacks'. Leanne Kelsey is a hack – looking for a fast-selling, hard-hitting story which will make her rich. But she has her uses… to the author!

As the story builds to its climax, her character and motivation add much to the tension of the novel.

Stop press

There are five 'Wh' questions a good journalist must answer as they track a story:
Who did it involve?
What happened?
Why did it happen?
Where did it take place?
When did it happen?

- Track how the tension rises in Chapters 43 and 44, by answering the questions above.
- Work out how Allen-Gray uses Leanne to increase the pace and excitement.

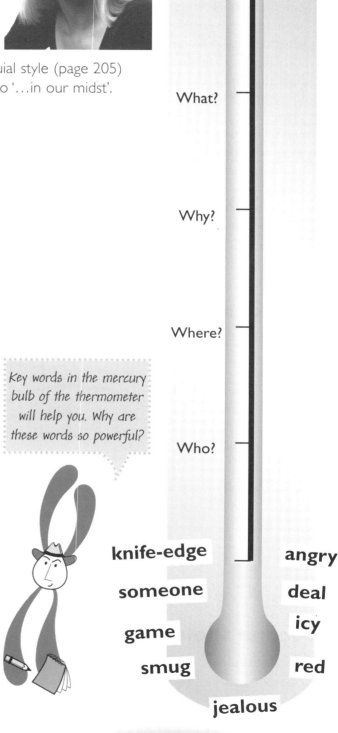

Key words in the mercury bulb of the thermometer will help you. Why are these words so powerful?

When? What? Why? Where? Who?

knife-edge angry
someone deal
game icy
smug red
jealous

Hackmail!

The tension is rising...

Reality check!

Of course, some readers love articles like Leanne's – they're extreme, entertaining and emotive.

But sometimes the truth is lost, people are hurt and some readers may even lose their grip on reality! Here's the full version of the letter Dominic finds in Chapter 41 in a leading newspaper.

> Dear Ed,
> I was amazed when your paper suggested that cloning will never happen. I have news for you – I am a clone and have been all my life. I was cloned at an early age and have only ever found it to be useful: I can be in two places at one time and will never die. At the age of 80, this is a comforting thought. I never listen to anyone who thinks such wonders of modern science are just fairytales – how could I agree with them when I am living proof that they are wrong! If you would like a picture of me as evidence of my existence, please do not hesitate ask.
> Yours,
> Mr T. J. Foxly
> Harmstead, Cornwall

The news on the street!

This newspaper story, which Dominic also finds in Chapter 41, is full of drama and conflict. Have a go at improvising this incident in small groups.
Plan how you will show:
- the persistence of the journalists
- the anger of the general public
- the fear and confusion of the children.

You might like to build your drama around freeze frames or a TV news bulletin.

Model Family!

Ex-model, Krishniana Dressart, and her tycoon husband attempted to go into hiding this morning. They were trying to evade the press and public angered at the revelation that they wanted a cloned daughter. Three years ago, they approached Wishart, now executed, to have Krishniana cloned. But their hopes were dashed as the plan was discovered.

Today, the family was pushed and shoved by jeering crowds as they struggled into their car. The three children – all boys – pushed their way through, but became increasingly distressed, the smallest of them, aged six, crying out to his mother as she was separated from him in the crush. The oldest brother, Benjamin, tried to protect him, but the little boy was grabbed by a large, red-faced woman who screamed at him, 'Are you a clone too?'

Unique

Pathways... to Another Good Read

Thematically-linked texts
Pre-1960

Twelfth Night by William Shakespeare (1601)
ISBN 0-19-832019-1
Comic-tragic events as separated twins make their endearing journey to a happy reunion.

Frankenstein by Mary Shelley (1918)
ISBN 0-19-283366-9
A Gothic quest for the secret of life itself, unfolding to a horrific climax as the inventive Dr Victor Frankenstein tries desperately to control the monster he has created.

Brave New World by Aldous Huxley (1932)
ISBN 0-09-945816-0
Set in a future where children are processed genetically in bottles rather than conceived naturally. We follow the ultimately sad and cautionary tale of John – a circus freak.

Nineteen Eighty-Four by George Orwell (1949)
ISBN 0-14-012671-6
Living in a future military state, Winston struggles to maintain his identity and independence and pays the ultimate price.

Four-Sided Triangle by William F. Temple (1952)
ISBN 1-58-715217-7
Two men, one woman and a machine that can copy anything… or anyone! This is the story of how two men and one woman find a solution to the eternal love triangle with a machine that will reproduce anything.

Post-1960

Gor Saga: First Born by Maureen Duffy (1981)
ISBN 0-41-319760-3
Set in the near future, this book tells the tale of a rich scientist, Norman Forester, who inseminates a gorilla with his own sperm. He then uses Gor – the resulting 'son' – as the basis for an extended laboratory experiment.

Complementary non-fiction

Who's Afraid of Human Cloning? by Gregory Pence (1998)
ISBN 0-84-768782-1
A clear, concise and compelling argument which advocates human cloning.

Cloning: For and Against, Vol 3 by Rantala and Milgram (1999)
ISBN 0-81-269375-2
A collection of essays and articles discussing this issue.

The Second Creation by Wilmut and Tudge (2000)
ISBN 0-74-725930-5
Professor Wilmut cloned the first mammal, Dolly the sheep, and here examines the history and science behind cloning.